ELIZABETH II

Zoo Licensing Act 1981

1981 CHAPTER 37

An Act to regulate by licence the conduct of zoos.

[27th July 1981]

B E IT ENACTED by the Queen's most Excellent Majesty, by and with the advice and consent of the Lords Spiritual and Temporal, and Commons, in this present Parliament assembled, and by the authority of the same, as follows:—

Licences

1.—(1) Subject to this section it is unlawful to operate a zoo to which this Act applies except under the authority of a licence issued under this Act by the local authority for the area within which the whole or the major part of the zoo is situated.

(2) In this Act "zoo" means an establishment where wild animals (as defined by section 21) are kept for exhibition to the public otherwise than for purposes of a circus (as so defined) and otherwise than in a pet shop (as so defined) ; and this Act applies to any zoo to which members of the public have access, with or without charge for admission, on more than seven days in any period of 12 consecutive months.

(3) The local authorities for the purposes of this Act are—

(*a*) in England and Wales, the district councils, the councils of London boroughs and the Common Council of the City of London ;

(*b*) in Scotland, the islands councils and district councils.

(4) In relation to zoos in operation before the commencement of this Act this section and section 2 have effect subject to the provisions of section 20.

Application
for licence.

2.—(1) An application to the local authority for a licence for a zoo shall not be entertained by the local authority unless, at least two months before making it, the applicant has given notice in writing to the local authority of his intention to make the application, has published notice of that intention in one local newspaper circulating in the locality and one newspaper with a national circulation and has exhibited a copy of that notice at the site and the said notice shall state that the notice to the local authority may be inspected as provided by subsection (3).

(2) Any notice given or published under subsection (1) must identify the situation of the zoo for which the application is to be made; and the notice to the local authority must specify—

    (a) the kinds of animals listed in taxonomic category of Order and approximate number of each group kept or to be kept for exhibition on the premises and the arrangements for their accommodation, maintenance and wellbeing;

    (b) the approximate numbers and categories of staff employed or to be employed in the zoo;

    (c) the approximate number of visitors and motor vehicles for which accommodation is or is to be provided;

    (d) the approximate number and position of the means of access provided or to be provided to the premises.

(3) Any notice given to the local authority under this section shall, until the disposal of the application to which it relates, be kept available by the authority at their offices for public inspection free of charge at reasonable hours.

Consideration
of application.

3.—(1) On the consideration of an application for a licence the local authority shall take into account any representations made by or on behalf of any of the persons mentioned in subsection (2).

(2) The persons are:—

    (a) the applicant;

    (b) the chief officer of police (or in Scotland the chief constable) for any area in which the whole or any part of the zoo is situated;

    (c) any authority discharging, in any area in which the whole or any part of the zoo is situated, the functions of fire authority under the Fire Services Act 1947;

    (d) the governing body of any national institution concerned with the operation of zoos;

    (e) where part of the zoo is not situated in the area of the local authority with power to grant the licence, a

1947 c. 41.

Zoo Licensing Act 1981

CHAPTER 37

ARRANGEMENT OF SECTIONS

A

Supplemental

planning authority for the area in which the part is situated (other than a county planning authority or the Greater London Council);

(*f*) any person alleging that the establishment or continuance of the zoo would injuriously affect the health or safety of persons living in the neighbourhood of the zoo;

(*g*) any other person whose representations might, in the opinion of the local authority, show grounds on which the authority has a power or duty to refuse to grant a licence.

4.—(1) Before granting or refusing to grant a licence for a zoo, the local authority shall— Grant or refusal of licence.

(*a*) consider inspectors' reports made in pursuance of inspections of the zoo under this Act, or

(*b*) if no inspection of the zoo has been made under this Act, consult such persons on the list as the Secretary of State nominates for the purposes of this section.

(2) The local authority shall refuse to grant a licence for a zoo if they are satisfied that the establishment or continuance of the zoo would injuriously affect the health or safety of persons living in the neighbourhood of the zoo, or seriously affect the preservation of law and order.

(3) The local authority may refuse to grant a licence for a zoo if they are not satisfied that the standards of accommodation. staffing or management are adequate for the proper care and wellbeing of the animals or any of them or otherwise for the proper conduct of the zoo.

(4) The local authority may also refuse to grant a licence if—

(*a*) the applicant, or

(*b*) (where the applicant is a body corporate) the body or any director, manager, secretary or other similar officer of the body, or

(*c*) any person employed as a keeper in the zoo,

has been convicted of an offence under this Act or under any of the enactments mentioned in. subsection (5) or of any other offence involving the ill-treatment of animals.

(5) The enactments are—

the Protection of Animals Acts 1911 to 1964;
the Protection of Animals (Scotland) Acts 1912 to 1964;
the Pet Animals Act 1951; 1951 c. 35.
the Protection of Birds Acts 1954 to 1967;
the Animal Boarding Establishments Act 1963; 1963 c. 43.

the Riding Establishments Acts 1964 and 1970;

1973 c. 60.   the Breeding of Dogs Act 1973;

1975 c. 48.   the Conservation of Wild Creatures and Wild Plants Act 1975;

1976 c. 38.   the Dangerous Wild Animals Act 1976;

1976 c. 72.   the Endangered Species (Import and Export) Act 1976.

(6) If the local authority are not satisfied that any planning permission required under Part III of the Town and Country Planning Act 1971 or under the Town and Country Planning (Scotland) Act 1972, for the establishment of the zoo or for the continuance of the zoo during the period for which the licence would be in force, has been, or is deemed to be, granted, they shall either refuse to grant the licence or grant the licence but suspend its operation until the local planning authority within the meaning of the said Act of 1971 or, as the case may be, 1972 have notified the local authority that any such planning permission has been or is deemed to be granted.

1971 c. 78.
1972 c. 52.

(7) Except as provided by this section the local authority shall not refuse to grant a licence pursuant to an application and if they do refuse to grant it they shall send to the applicant by post a written statement of the grounds of their refusal.

(8) When a licence is granted the local authority shall send it to the applicant by post and the licence or a copy of it shall be publicly displayed at each public entrance to the zoo.

Period and conditions of licence.

5.—(1) An original licence granted under this Act shall be granted for a period of four years beginning with the date specified in the licence as that on which it is granted or any later date specified in the licence as that on which the licence is to commence.

(2) A fresh licence granted under this Act to the holder of an existing licence shall be granted for a period of six years beginning with the end of the period of the existing licence.

(3) Any licence under this Act may be granted subject to such conditions as the local authority think necessary or desirable for ensuring the proper conduct of the zoo during the period of the licence, including conditions relating to the following—

(a) precautions to be taken against the escape of animals, and steps to be taken in the event of any escape or unauthorised release;

(b) records to be kept of the numbers of different animals, of acquisitions, births, deaths, disposals or escapes of animals, of the causes of any such deaths, and of the health of animals;

(c) insurance against liability for damage caused by animals.

(4) In deciding what (if any) conditions to attach to a licence, a local authority shall have regard to any standards specified by the Secretary of State under section 9 and sent by him to the authority.

(5) A local authority shall attach to a licence any condition which the Secretary of State directs them to attach.

(6) The authority shall not attach to a licence any condition inconsistent with one they are so directed to attach.

(7) The authority shall not attach to a licence a condition which relates only or primarily to the health, safety or welfare of persons working in the zoo.

6.—(1) Where application for the renewal of an existing licence is made to the local authority not later than six months before the end of the period of the licence or such shorter time as the local authority may in special circumstances allow the local authority may either— Renewal of licence.

   (*a*) extend the period of the existing licence ; or
   (*b*) direct the applicant to apply for a fresh licence in accordance with section 2.

(2) Where application for a fresh licence is made by the holder of an existing licence, the existing licence shall, if the application is made before the end of the period of that licence or within six months after notice of a direction given to the applicant under subsection (1)(*b*), continue in force until the application is disposed of or withdrawn and, if the application is refused, for a further period of six months.

(3) Any extension of the period of an existing licence under subsection (1) (*a*) shall be granted for a period of six years beginning with the end of the period of the existing licence ; and the local authority shall take reasonable steps to secure that the holder of the licence is notified in writing of the extension.

(4) The local authority shall give notice to the holder of any licence granted by that authority, not later than nine months before the end of the period of the licence, of the latest date on which application for renewal may be made under this section.

7.—(1) A licence for a zoo may with the approval of the local authority be transferred to another person, and in that case the transferee shall become the holder of the licence from the date which application for renewal may be made under this section. Transfer, transmission and surrender of licence.

(2) On the death of the holder of a licence, the personal representatives of the deceased are deemed to be the holders of the licence during the period of three months after the death or such longer period as the local authority may approve.

(3) The holder of a licence may at any time surrender it to the local authority who shall thereupon cancel the licence.

Secretary of State's functions

Secretary of
State's list.

8.—(1) The Secretary of State shall, after consultation with the presidents of the British Veterinary Association, the National Federation of Zoological Gardens and the National Zoological Association and with such other persons as he thinks fit, compile a list consisting of two parts, the first part containing the names of veterinary surgeons and veterinary practitioners falling within subsection (2) and the second part containing the names of persons falling within subsection (3).

(2) The surgeons and practitioners shall have experience of animals of kinds which are kept in zoos or which in the Secretary of State's opinion might be so kept.

(3) Each of the persons shall be competent in the Secretary of State's opinion to do all the following, namely, to inspect animals in zoos, to advise on keeping them and on their welfare, and to advise on the management of zoos generally.

(4) A person's name may be contained in both the first and the second parts of the list.

(5) After such consultation, the Secretary of State may vary the list by adding names or deleting them (or both).

(6) Persons on the list may charge the licensing authority such amounts in respect of their services and expenses as the Secretary of State may from time to time determine with the approval of the Minister for the Civil Service.

Secretary of
State's
standards.

9. After consulting such persons on the list and such other persons as he thinks fit, the Secretary of State may from time to time specify standards of modern zoo practice, that is, standards with respect to the management of zoos and the animals in them.

Inspections

Periodical
inspections.

10.—(1) The local authority shall carry out periodical inspections in accordance with this section of any zoo for which a licence granted by that authority is in force.

(2) Before any such inspection the local authority shall, after consultation with the operator of the zoo, give him at least twenty-eight days notice of the date upon which it is proposed to carry it out.

(3) Inspections under this section shall be made at the following times—

    (*a*) in the case of an original licence, during the first year and not later than six months before the end of the fourth year of the period of the licence;

(b) in the case of a renewed licence or fresh licence granted to the holder of an existing licence, during the third year and not later than six months before the end of the sixth year of the period of that licence.

(4) The following provisions apply to any inspection to be carried out under this section:—

(a) the inspection shall be conducted by the following inspectors, namely—

(i) not more than three appointed by the local authority, being persons who appear to the authority to be competent for the purpose, at least one of whom shall be a veterinary surgeon or veterinary practitioner ; and

(ii) two nominated after consultation with the local authority by the Secretary of State from the list, one from the first part of the list and one from the second ;

and the names of all persons inspecting shall be notified to the operator of the zoo ;

(b) the operator may give notice to the local authority of objection to any one or more of the inspectors, and the local authority or the Secretary of State as appropriate may if they think fit give effect to any such objection ;

(c) representatives of the operator not exceeding three in number may accompany the inspectors on the inspection ; and the inspectors may require the attendance of any veterinary surgeon or veterinary practitioner employed in or retained by or for the purposes of the zoo ;

(d) the inspection shall extend to all features of the zoo directly or indirectly relevant to the health, welfare and safety of the public and the animals, including measures for the prevention of the escape of animals ;

(e) the inspectors shall require the production of all records kept by the operator in pursuance of conditions of the licence under section 5(3)(b) and the operator shall produce the records.

(5) The inspectors shall send their report to the local authority, and the report may include advice on the keeping of records and recommendations for any practicable improvements designed to bring any features of the zoo up to the normal standards of modern zoo practice ; and for this purpose the inspectors shall have regard to any standards known to them which have been specified by the Secretary of State under section 9.

(6) Any disagreement between the inspectors over recommendations to be made in their report relating to the welfare of the animals or any of them may be referred to the Secretary of State, who may, after consultation with such persons on the list as he thinks fit, give such guidance as he thinks proper in regard to the recommendations to be made.

(7) Within one month after receiving the report of the inspection the local authority shall send a copy to the operator of the zoo and give him an opportunity to comment on it.

Special inspections.

11.—(1) The local authority may at any time carry out a special inspection of a zoo for which a licence granted by them is in force if they consider it appropriate to do so having regard to—

   (*a*) any periodical report on the zoo made to them pursuant to section 10 ; or

   (*b*) any representations made to them on behalf of a properly constituted body concerned with any aspect of the management of zoos or the welfare of animals ; or

   (*c*) any report on the zoo made to them pursuant to an inspection under the provisions of section 12 ; or

   (*d*) any other circumstances which in their opinion call for investigation.

(2) A special inspection under this section shall be conducted by persons who appear to the local authority to be competent for the purpose and who are authorised by the authority to conduct the inspection.

(3) Where the purpose of the inspection relates to the health of animals, the inspectors shall include (or, if one, the inspector shall be) a veterinary surgeon or veterinary practitioner with experience of animals of kinds kept in the zoo.

(4) On appointing persons under subsection (2), the authority shall communicate to them and to the operator of the zoo the purpose and scope of the inspection.

(5) Paragraphs (*c*) to (*e*) of subsection (4) and subsections (5) to (7) of section 10 apply to a special inspection as they apply to a periodical inspection except that the references in subsections (4)(*d*), (4)(*e*) and (5) to features and records and improvements are references only to features and records and improvements relevant to the purpose and scope of the special inspection.

Informal inspections.

12.—(1) Without prejudice to sections 10 and 11, the local authority shall make such arrangements as they think fit to ensure that any zoo for which a licence granted by that authority is in force is inspected informally by an inspector once in any calendar year in which no inspection is made under those sections.

(2) The inspector shall be appointed by the authority and shall be a person appearing to the authority to be competent for the purpose of the inspection.

Special cases

13.—(1) When a local authority is the owner of a zoo to which Local this Act applies, this Act shall apply with the following additions authority and modifications. zoos.

(2) As soon as practicable after granting a licence for the zoo, or extending the period of a licence, or receiving an inspectors' report made in pursuance of an inspection of the zoo under this Act, the authority shall send to the Secretary of State a copy of the licence, or notification in writing of the extension, or a copy of the report (as the case may be).

(3) The authority shall send with the copy of the report any comments on it which they may have.

(4) The Secretary of State (instead of the authority) shall have power, after giving the holder of the licence an opportunity to be heard, to revoke the licence on any of the grounds mentioned in section 17(1)(a) to (d), and references in those paragraphs to the authority shall be construed as references to the Secretary of State.

(5) Subsections (2) and (3) of section 17 apply for the purposes of subsection (4) above as if references to the authority were references to the Secretary of State, and section 18 applies for those purposes with the appropriate modifications.

14.—(1) If the local authority with power to grant a licence Dispensation for a zoo inform the Secretary of State that in their opinion for particular a direction should be made under this subsection because of zoos. the small size of the zoo or the small number of the kinds of animal kept there, he may, after consulting such persons on the list as he thinks fit, direct—

    (a) that this Act shall not apply to that zoo ; or

    (b) that sections 10 and 11 or either of them shall not apply thereto.

(2) If the operator of a zoo informs the Secretary of State that in his opinion a direction should be made under this subsection because the number of inspectors provided for by section 10(4)(a) is too large for the zoo (having regard to the small size of the zoo or the small number of the kinds of animal kept

there), the Secretary of State may, after consulting the local authority with power to grant a licence for the zoo and such persons on the list as he thinks fit, direct—

    (a) that in the application of this Act to the zoo, section 10(4)(a) and (b) shall not apply ; and

    (b) that, instead, any inspection to be carried out under section 10 shall be conducted by such inspector or inspectors as the Secretary of State appoints.

(3) Any direction made under subsection (1) or (2) may be revoked or varied by a further direction of the Secretary of State made after he has consulted the local authority and such persons on the list as he thinks fit.

(4) While a direction under subsection (1) has effect, this Act, or sections 10 and 11, or either of them, shall not apply to the zoo (depending on the terms of the direction and any variation made by a further direction under subsection (3)).

(5) While a direction under subsection (2) has effect, this Act shall apply to the zoo with the modifications specified in the direction (subject to any variation made by a further direction under subsection (3)).

(6) The Secretary of State shall take reasonable steps to secure that the local authority and any person who operates the zoo are notified in writing of any direction made under subsection (1), (2) or (3).

Fees etc.

Fees and other charges.   **15.**—(1) Subject to this section, the local authority may charge such fees as they may determine in respect of—

    (a) applications for the grant, renewal or transfer of licences ;

    (b) the grant, renewal or transfer of licences ;

and may charge to the operators of zoos such sums as they may determine on account of expenses incurred by them upon inspections under sections 10 to 12.

(2) Any fee charged under paragraph (a) of subsection (1) in respect of an application shall be treated as paid on account of the fee charged under paragraph (b) on the grant, renewal or transfer applied for.

(3) In respect of any fee or other sum charged under this section, the local authority may, if so requested by the operator, accept payment by instalments.

(4) Any fee or other charge payable under this section by any person shall be recoverable by the local authority as a debt due from him to them.

(5) The local authority shall secure that the amount of all the fees and other sums charged by them under this section in a year is sufficient to cover the amount of expenditure incurred by the authority in the year by virtue of this Act.

Enforcement

16.—(1) At any time after the grant of a licence under this Act, it may be altered by the local authority if in their opinion it is necessary or desirable to do so for ensuring the proper conduct of the zoo during the period of the licence (whether their opinion arises from an inspectors' report or an alteration of standards specified under section 9 or otherwise).

Power to alter licences.

(2) Before exercising the power under subsection (1), the local authority shall give the holder of the licence an opportunity to make representations.

(3) If, at any time after the grant of a licence under this Act, the Secretary of State directs a local authority to alter the licence, the authority shall give effect to the direction within a reasonable time.

(4) An alteration under this section may be made by varying, cancelling or attaching conditions or by a combination of any of those methods.

(5) The authority shall secure that the terms of any condition attached to a licence are not inconsistent with the terms of a condition attached or varied in pursuance of a direction of the Secretary of State.

(6) No alteration made under subsection (1) or in pursuance of a direction under subsection (3) shall have effect until written notification of it has been received by the holder of the licence; and this subsection is without prejudice to section 18(7).

17.—(1) The local authority may, after giving the holder an opportunity to be heard, revoke a licence for a zoo granted by them under this Act—

Revocation of licence.

    (*a*) if any reasonable requirements relating to the premises or conduct of the zoo notified by them to the holder in consequence of the report of any inspection under this Act are not complied with within such time as is reasonable in the circumstances;

    (*b*) if they are satisfied that the zoo has been conducted in a disorderly manner or so as to cause a nuisance, or in breach of any conditions of the licence;

    (*c*) if the holder (or, where the holder is a body corporate, the body or any director, manager, secretary or other similar officer of the body) is convicted of any offence mentioned in section 4(4);

(d) if any person who, to the knowledge of the holder, has been so convicted is employed as a keeper in the zoo.

(2) No licence may be revoked under subsection (1)(a) or (b) on grounds involving the care or treatment of animals unless the authority first consults such persons on the list as the Secretary of State may nominate for the purposes of this subsection.

(3) The local authority shall take reasonable steps to secure that the holder of the licence is notified in writing of their decision to revoke the licence.

Appeals.

18.—(1) A person aggrieved by the refusal to grant a licence, by any condition attached to a licence, by any variation or cancellation of a condition or by the revocation of a licence may appeal—

(a) in England and Wales, to a magistrates' court acting for the petty sessions area in which the zoo is situated ;

(b) in Scotland, by summary application to the sheriff.

(2) Any such appeal shall be brought within twenty-one days from the date on which the person wishing to appeal receives written notification of the authority's decision to refuse to grant a licence, to revoke a licence, to attach a condition (whether on the grant of the licence or later) or to vary or cancel a condition, as the case may be ; but an appeal may be brought under this section whether or not the authority's decision was made in pursuance of a direction of the Secretary of State under this Act.

(3) On an appeal under this section to a magistrates' court, the court may confirm, vary or reverse the local authority's decision and generally give such directions as it thinks proper, having regard to the provisions of this Act.

(4) On an appeal under this section to the sheriff, he shall have power (without prejudice to any other power which he may have) to confirm, vary or reverse the local authority's decision and to award such expenses as he thinks fit.

(5) The procedure on an appeal to a magistrates' court under this section shall be by way of complaint for an order, and the

1980 c. 43.

Magistrates' Courts Act 1980 shall apply to the proceedings.

(6) The decision of the sheriff on an appeal under this section **shall be final.**

(7) In so far as a condition attached to a licence (whether on its grant or later), or the variation of a condition, imposes a requirement on the holder of the licence to carry out works he would not otherwise be required to carry out, the condition or the variation shall not have effect—

(*a*) during the period within which the holder is entitled to appeal against the attachment or variation, or

(*b*) where such an appeal is brought within that period, during the period before the appeal is determined or abandoned.

(8) A licence revoked under section 17 shall be deemed to continue in force—

(*a*) if no appeal is brought under this section within the time mentioned in subsection (2), until the expiration of the period of six months commencing with the expiration of that time ; or

(*b*) if an appeal is so brought, until the determination or abandonment of the appeal (but without prejudice to the licence continuing in force further by virtue of the court's or sheriff's decision or of subsection (9)).

(9) If, on an appeal brought under this section, the court or the sheriff confirms a revocation under section 17, the licence shall be deemed to continue in force for a further period of six months commencing with the date of the confirmation.

19.—(1) If a zoo is operated without a licence in contravention of this Act, the operator is guilty of an offence. Offences and penalties.

(2) If the operator of a zoo fails without reasonable excuse to comply with any condition for the time being attached to a licence for the zoo granted under this Act and held by him, he is guilty of an offence.

(3) Any person who intentionally obstructs an inspector acting pursuant to this Act is guilty of an offence.

(4) A person guilty of an offence under this section is liable on summary conviction to a fine not exceeding £500 for an offence under subsection (1) or (2) and £200 for an offence under subsection (3).

(5) Where an offence under this section committed by a body corporate is proved to have been committed with the consent or connivance of, or to have been attributed to any neglect on the part of, any director, manager, secretary or any other similar officer of the body corporate, or any person who was purporting

to act in any such capacity, he, as well as the body corporate, is guilty of that offence and liable to be proceeded against and punished accordingly.

Supplemental

Transitory provision for existing zoos.

20.—(1) A person who immediately before the date of the commencement of this Act was operating a zoo on any premises may continue to operate that zoo on those premises without a licence under this Act—

(a) during the period of six months beginning with that date ; and

(b) if within that period application is made for a licence, until that application is finally disposed of or withdrawn and, if the application is refused, for a further period of six months.

(2) In the case of an application made as mentioned in subsection (1)(b), notice of intention to make the application shall not be required under section 2, but the application shall specify all such particulars as would be required to be included in a notice to the local authority under that section.

(3) On any such application the local authority shall carry out an inspection of the zoo in accordance with the provisions of section 10 before deciding whether to grant or refuse the licence, and may, if the licence is granted, grant it subject to such conditions as may be specified in the report of the inspectors.

(4) If the licence is granted—

(a) the inspection required by this section is in lieu of the first inspection under paragraph (a) of subsection (3) of section 10 ;

(b) it shall be granted for a period of four years beginning with the date on which the licence is granted.

Interpretation.

21.—(1) In this Act—

" animals " means animals of the classes Mammalia, Aves, Reptilia, Amphibia, Pisces and Insecta and any other multi cellular organism that is not a plant or a fungus and " wild animals " means animals not normally domesticated in Great Britain ;

" circus " means a place where animals are kept or introduced wholly or mainly for the purpose of performing tricks or manoeuvres at that place ;

" keeper " includes any person employed under the directions of a keeper ;

" the list " means the list compiled by the Secretary of State under section 8 ;

" pet shop " means premises for whose keeping as a pet shop a licence is in force, or is required, under the Pet Animals Act 1951 ;   1951 c. 35,

" taxonomic category " means a group or assemblage of species recognised as an entity in scientific classification ;

" zoo " has the meaning assigned by section 1(2).

(2) Nothing in this Act and nothing done under it shall prejudice or affect the operation of any of the relevant statutory provisions (whenever made) as defined in Part I of the Health and Safety at Work etc. Act 1974.   1974 c. 37.

22.—(1) The Dangerous Wild Animals Act 1976 shall be amended as follows—   Consequential amendments.

    (*a*) in section 5, for paragraph (1) there shall be substituted   1976 c. 38.
" (1) a zoo within the meaning of the Zoo Licensing Act 1981 for which a licence is in force (or is not for the time being required) under that Act " ;

    (*b*) in section 7(4) the definition of zoological garden shall be omitted.

(2) For the purpose of the said Act an animal shall be treated as kept in a zoo when it is elsewhere in the personal possession of the operator of the zoo, or of competent persons acting on his behalf.

23.—(1) This Act may be cited as the Zoo Licensing Act 1981.   Short title, commencement and extent.

(2) This Act shall come into operation on such day as the Secretary of State may by order made by statutory instrument appoint.

(3) This Act does not extend to Northern Ireland.

Printed in the UK by The Stationery Office Limited
under the authority and superintendence of Carol Tullo, Controller of
Her Majesty's Stationery Office and Queen's Printer of Acts of Parliament

1st Impression August 1981
2nd Impression October 1997

Printed in the United Kingdom for The Stationery Office
Dd 759832 10/97 1731 56219

ISBN 0-10-543781-6

£3.80

9 780105 437819 >